My Journal

on my way to a

NEW & BETTER

··

/ME/

ISBN: 978-1985865181

week 1	1	2	3	4	5	6	7
week 2	8	9	10	11	12	13	14
week 3	15	16	17	18	19	20	21
week 4	22	23	24	25	26	27	28
week 5	29	30	31	32	33	34	35
week 6	36	37	38	39	40	41	42
week 7	43	44	45	46	47	48	49
week 8	50	51	52	53	54	55	56
week 9	57	58	59	60	61	62	63
week 10	64	65	66	67	68	69	70
week 11	71	72	73	74	75	76	77
week 12	78	79	80	81	82	83	84
week 13	85	86	87	88	89	90	

30 Days
to form a
NEW HABIT

Determine your new
DAILY GOALS & HABITS:

_____
_____
_____
_____

Cross a BIG X
over each day you
ACCOMPLISH
your new habit(s)

60 Days
to enjoy a
CHANGING YOU

Time to
CELEBRATE
your progress

90 Days
to welcome your
NEW ME

☀ 20 THINGS to start doing now

1. Keep a food journal. If you bite it write it. 📖

2. Drink a lot of water and green tea.

3. Eat fruits and vegetables (more greens) + natural food.

4. Avoid processed food.

5. Go for a walk / bike ride.

6. Ditch the elevator for the stairs.

7. Dance, dance, dance it out!

8. Stretch daily to increase flexibility.

9. Go outside more.

10. Try yoga or meditation.

11. Go to bed earlier.

12. Wear clothes that make you happy.

13. Stop thinking negative thoughts about yourself or anyone else.

14. Do not judge yourself.

15. Do not compare yourself to others.

16. Throw away things you don't need.

17. Enjoy little things in life.

18. Next time you want to give up remember why you started.

19. Remember that all your efforts now will surely pay in the end.

20. Do it badly, do it slowly, do it inconsistently, do it any way you have to, but **do it anyway**. And then say hello to your NEW ME!

DAY 1 : My Starting Point

chest [1] ....

waist [2] ....

hips [3] ....

thigh [4] ....

calf [5] ....

weight ....

MY GOALS:

I am gorgeous the way I am! ... but here is what I'd like to improve: ....

....

....

....

DAY 1

BREAKFAST

1 egg + cheese
1/4 tomatoe
5 pcs. of salami
coffe w/milk

LUNCH

yogurt + my granola
+ blueberries

1 tomatoe + 1 row of
"salami"

DINNER

SNACKS

nuts — | | | | | |

WATER

▯▯▯▯▯▯▯▯▯▯▯▯▯▯▯▯▯▯▯▯

SLEEP TIME

EXERCISE / ACTIVITY

**How I feel today about my
food & exercise**

○ ☹   ○ ☹
○ 😐   ○ 😐
○ ☺   ○ ☺

CRAVINGS / RESPONSE

Something to make tomorrow better:

DAY

BREAKFAST

LUNCH

DINNER

SNACKS

WATER

SLEEP TIME

EXERCISE / ACTIVITY

How I feel today about my
food & exercise

o ☹   o ☹

o 😐   o 😐

o ☺   o ☺

CRAVINGS / RESPONSE

Something to make tomorrow better:

DAY ③

BREAKFAST

....

....

....

....

SNACKS

....

....

....

LUNCH

....

....

....

....

....

....

....

....

DINNER

....

....

....

....

....

....

....

....

WATER

🥛🥛🥛🥛🥛🥛🥛🥛🥛🥛🥛🥛🥛🥛🥛🥛🥛🥛

EXERCISE / ACTIVITY

....

....

....

....

CRAVINGS / RESPONSE

....

....

SLEEP TIME

....

How I feel today about my
food & exercise

○ ☹   ○ ☹

○ 😐   ○ 😐

○ ☺   ○ ☺

Something to make tomorrow better:

....

....

DAY  4

BREAKFAST   LUNCH   DINNER

SNACKS

WATER   SLEEP TIME

EXERCISE / ACTIVITY

How I feel today about my
food   &   exercise

○ ☹   ○ ☹
○ 😐   ○ 😐
○ ☺   ○ ☺

CRAVINGS / RESPONSE

Something to make tomorrow better:

DAY (5)

BREAKFAST

....
....
....
....

LUNCH

....

DINNER

....
....
....
....

SNACKS

....
....
....
....

....
....
....
....

....
....
....
....

WATER

⊔⊔⊔⊔⊔⊔⊔⊔⊔⊔⊔⊔⊔⊔⊔⊔⊔⊔⊔⊔

SLEEP TIME

....

EXERCISE / ACTIVITY

....
....
....
....

How I feel today about my
food   &   exercise

○ ☹   ○ ☹

○ 😐   ○ 😐

○ ☺   ○ ☺

CRAVINGS / RESPONSE

....
....

Something to make tomorrow better:

....
....

DAY  6

BREAKFAST   LUNCH   DINNER

....
....
....
....

SNACKS
....
....
....
....

WATER   SLEEP TIME
\[glasses of water icons\]   ....

EXERCISE / ACTIVITY
                                                  How I feel today about my
....   food   &   exercise
....   ○ ☹   ○ ☹
....   ○ 😐   ○ 😐
....   ○ 🙂   ○ 🙂

CRAVINGS / RESPONSE
....
....

Something to make tomorrow better:
....
....

DAY

BREAKFAST

LUNCH

DINNER

SNACKS

WATER

SLEEP TIME

EXERCISE / ACTIVITY

How I feel today about my
food   &   exercise

○ ☹   ○ ☹

○ 😐   ○ 😐

○ ☺   ○ ☺

CRAVINGS / RESPONSE

Something to make tomorrow better:

DAY (8)

BREAKFAST

....
....
....
....
....

LUNCH

....
....
....
....
....

DINNER

....
....
....
....
....

SNACKS

....
....
....
....

WATER

🥛🥛🥛🥛🥛🥛🥛🥛🥛🥛🥛🥛🥛🥛🥛🥛🥛

EXERCISE / ACTIVITY

....
....
....
....
....

CRAVINGS / RESPONSE

SLEEP TIME

....

How I feel today about my
food & exercise

o (☹)   o (☹)
o (😐)   o (😐)
o (☺)   o (☺)

Something to make tomorrow better:

....
....

DAY (9)

BREAKFAST

_____
_____
_____
_____

SNACKS

_____
_____
_____

LUNCH

_____
_____
_____
_____
_____
_____
_____
_____

DINNER

_____
_____
_____
_____
_____
_____
_____
_____

WATER

🥛🥛🥛🥛🥛🥛🥛🥛🥛🥛🥛🥛🥛🥛🥛🥛🥛🥛🥛🥛

SLEEP TIME

_____

EXERCISE / ACTIVITY

_____
_____
_____
_____

How I feel today about my food & exercise

food:
○ 🙁
○ 😐
○ 🙂

exercise:
○ 🙁
○ 😐
○ 🙂

CRAVINGS / RESPONSE

_____

Something to make tomorrow better:

_____
_____

DAY

BREAKFAST   LUNCH   DINNER

....

....

....

....

SNACKS   ....

....

....

....

WATER   SLEEP TIME

[16 water glasses]   ....

EXERCISE / ACTIVITY

....   How I feel today about my
....   food & exercise
....
....   ○ :(○ :(

....   ○ :| ○ :|

CRAVINGS / RESPONSE   ○ :)   ○ :)

....

....

Something to make tomorrow better:

....

....

DAY (11)

BREAKFAST

....
....
....
....

SNACKS

....
....
....

LUNCH

....
....
....
....
....
....
....

DINNER

....
....
....
....

WATER

⊔⊔⊔⊔⊔⊔⊔⊔⊔⊔⊔⊔⊔⊔⊔⊔⊔⊔⊔

EXERCISE / ACTIVITY

....
....
....
....
....

SLEEP TIME

....

How I feel today about my food & exercise

○ ☹   ○ ☹
○ 😐   ○ 😐
○ ☺   ○ ☺

CRAVINGS / RESPONSE

....
....

Something to make tomorrow better:

....
....

DAY (12)

BREAKFAST

LUNCH

DINNER

SNACKS

WATER

🥛🥛🥛🥛🥛🥛🥛🥛🥛🥛🥛🥛🥛🥛🥛🥛

SLEEP TIME

EXERCISE / ACTIVITY

How I feel today about my
food & exercise

○ 🙁   ○ 🙁

○ 😐   ○ 😐

○ 🙂   ○ 🙂

CRAVINGS / RESPONSE

Something to make tomorrow better:

DAY (13)

BREAKFAST

_____
_____
_____
_____
_____

SNACKS

_____
_____
_____

LUNCH

_____
_____
_____
_____
_____
_____
_____

DINNER

_____
_____
_____
_____
_____

WATER

ᗡᗡᗡᗡᗡᗡᗡᗡᗡᗡᗡᗡᗡᗡᗡᗡ

EXERCISE / ACTIVITY

_____
_____
_____
_____

SLEEP TIME

_____

How I feel today about my
food & exercise

○ :(○ :(
○ :| ○ :|
○ :)   ○ :)

CRAVINGS / RESPONSE

_____
_____

Something to make tomorrow better:

_____
_____

DAY (14)

BREAKFAST
....
....
....
....

SNACKS
....
....
....

LUNCH
....
....
....
....
....
....
....

DINNER
....
....
....
....
....
....

WATER

SLEEP TIME
....

EXERCISE / ACTIVITY
....
....
....
....

How I feel today about my
food   &   exercise

○ :(○ :(
○ :| ○ :|
○ :)   ○ :)

CRAVINGS / RESPONSE
....
....

Something to make tomorrow better:
....
....

DAY (15)

BREAKFAST

_____
_____
_____
_____

SNACKS

_____
_____
_____

LUNCH

_____
_____
_____
_____
_____
_____
_____

DINNER

_____
_____
_____
_____

WATER

🥛🥛🥛🥛🥛🥛🥛🥛🥛🥛🥛🥛🥛🥛🥛🥛

SLEEP TIME

_____

EXERCISE / ACTIVITY

_____
_____
_____
_____

How I feel today about my
food & exercise

o 🙁   o 🙁
o 😐   o 😐
o 🙂   o 🙂

CRAVINGS / RESPONSE

_____
_____

Something to make tomorrow better:

_____
_____

DAY (16)

BREAKFAST

LUNCH

DINNER

SNACKS

WATER

SLEEP TIME

EXERCISE / ACTIVITY

How I feel today about my
food & exercise

○ (☹)   ○ (☹)

○ (😐)   ○ (😐)

○ (☺)   ○ (☺)

CRAVINGS / RESPONSE

Something to make tomorrow better:

DAY (17)

BREAKFAST

....

....

....

....

LUNCH

....

....

....

....

DINNER

....

....

....

....

SNACKS

....

....

....

....

WATER

⊔⊔⊔⊔⊔⊔⊔⊔⊔⊔⊔⊔⊔⊔⊔⊔

SLEEP TIME

....

EXERCISE / ACTIVITY

....

....

....

....

How I feel today about my food & exercise

○ ☹   ○ ☹

○ 😐   ○ 😐

○ ☺   ○ ☺

CRAVINGS / RESPONSE

....

....

Something to make tomorrow better:

....

....

DAY (18)

BREAKFAST   LUNCH   DINNER

....

....

....

SNACKS   ....

....

....

....

WATER   SLEEP TIME

▽▽▽▽▽▽▽▽▽▽▽▽▽▽▽▽▽▽▽▽   ....

EXERCISE / ACTIVITY

                                                 How I feel today about my
....   food   &   exercise

....   ○ ☹   ○ ☹

....   ○ 😐   ○ 😐

....   ○ ☺   ○ ☺

CRAVINGS / RESPONSE

....

....

Something to make tomorrow better:

....

....

DAY (19)

BREAKFAST

LUNCH

DINNER

SNACKS

WATER

🥤🥤🥤🥤🥤🥤🥤🥤🥤🥤🥤🥤🥤🥤🥤🥤🥤

SLEEP TIME

EXERCISE / ACTIVITY

How I feel today about my
food & exercise

○ ☹   ○ ☹

○ 😐   ○ 😐

○ ☺   ○ ☺

CRAVINGS / RESPONSE

Something to make tomorrow better:

DAY

BREAKFAST   LUNCH   DINNER

....

....

....

SNACKS   ....

....

....

....

WATER   SLEEP TIME
   ....

EXERCISE / ACTIVITY

....   How I feel today about my
....   food   &   exercise
....
....   ○ ☹   ○ ☹

....   ○ 😐   ○ 😐

CRAVINGS / RESPONSE   ○ 🙂   ○ 🙂

....

....

Something to make tomorrow better:

....

....

DAY (21)

BREAKFAST

....

....

....

....

SNACKS

....

....

....

....

LUNCH

....

....

....

....

....

....

....

....

DINNER

....

....

....

....

....

....

....

....

WATER

🥛🥛🥛🥛🥛🥛🥛🥛🥛🥛🥛🥛🥛🥛🥛🥛🥛🥛

EXERCISE / ACTIVITY

....

....

....

....

CRAVINGS / RESPONSE

....

SLEEP TIME

....

How I feel today about my
food & exercise

○ 🙁   ○ 🙁

○ 😐   ○ 😐

○ 🙂   ○ 🙂

Something to make tomorrow better:

....

....

DAY

BREAKFAST   LUNCH   DINNER

SNACKS

WATER

SLEEP TIME

EXERCISE / ACTIVITY

How I feel today about my food & exercise

○ ☹   ○ ☹

○ 😐   ○ 😐

○ ☺   ○ ☺

CRAVINGS / RESPONSE

Something to make tomorrow better:

DAY  23

BREAKFAST

LUNCH

DINNER

SNACKS

WATER

🥛🥛🥛🥛🥛🥛🥛🥛🥛🥛🥛🥛🥛🥛🥛🥛

SLEEP TIME

EXERCISE / ACTIVITY

How I feel today about my
food & exercise

○ ☹   ○ ☹

○ 😐   ○ 😐

○ ☺   ○ ☺

CRAVINGS / RESPONSE

Something to make tomorrow better:

DAY  24

BREAKFAST   LUNCH   DINNER

SNACKS

WATER

🥛🥛🥛🥛🥛🥛🥛🥛🥛🥛🥛🥛🥛🥛🥛🥛

SLEEP TIME

EXERCISE / ACTIVITY

How I feel today about my
food & exercise

○ ☹   ○ ☹

○ 😐   ○ 😐

○ ☺   ○ ☺

CRAVINGS / RESPONSE

Something to make tomorrow better:

DAY

BREAKFAST   LUNCH   DINNER

SNACKS

WATER   SLEEP TIME

🥛🥛🥛🥛🥛🥛🥛🥛🥛🥛🥛🥛🥛🥛🥛🥛

EXERCISE / ACTIVITY

How I feel today about my
food   &   exercise

○ ☹   ○ ☹

○ 😐   ○ 😐

○ 🙂   ○ 🙂

CRAVINGS / RESPONSE

Something to make tomorrow better:

DAY

BREAKFAST   LUNCH   DINNER

SNACKS

WATER   SLEEP TIME

EXERCISE / ACTIVITY

How I feel today about my
food & exercise

○ ☹   ○ ☹

○ 😐   ○ 😐

○ 🙂   ○ 🙂

CRAVINGS / RESPONSE

Something to make tomorrow better:

DAY

BREAKFAST   LUNCH   DINNER

SNACKS

WATER   SLEEP TIME

EXERCISE / ACTIVITY

How I feel today about my
food & exercise

○ ☹   ○ ☹

○ 😐   ○ 😐

○ 🙂   ○ 🙂

CRAVINGS / RESPONSE

Something to make tomorrow better:

DAY  28

BREAKFAST	LUNCH	DINNER

SNACKS

WATER

SLEEP TIME

EXERCISE / ACTIVITY

How I feel today about my
food & exercise

○ ☹ ○ ☹

○ 😐 ○ 😐

○ ☺ ○ ☺

CRAVINGS / RESPONSE

Something to make tomorrow better:

DAY  29

BREAKFAST

LUNCH

DINNER

SNACKS

WATER

SLEEP TIME

EXERCISE / ACTIVITY

How I feel today about my food & exercise

○ (☹)   ○ (☹)

○ (😐)   ○ (😐)

○ (☺)   ○ (☺)

CRAVINGS / RESPONSE

Something to make tomorrow better:

DAY

BREAKFAST   LUNCH   DINNER

SNACKS

WATER   SLEEP TIME

EXERCISE / ACTIVITY

How I feel today about my
food   &   exercise

CRAVINGS / RESPONSE

Something to make tomorrow better:

DAY (31)

BREAKFAST

LUNCH

DINNER

SNACKS

WATER

WWWWWWWWWWWWWWWWWW

SLEEP TIME

EXERCISE / ACTIVITY

How I feel today about my
food   &   exercise

o ☹   o ☹

o 😐   o 😐

o ☺   o ☺

CRAVINGS / RESPONSE

Something to make tomorrow better:

DAY

BREAKFAST   LUNCH   DINNER

SNACKS

WATER   SLEEP TIME

EXERCISE / ACTIVITY

How I feel today about my
food & exercise

○ 🙁   ○ 🙁

○ 😐   ○ 😐

○ 🙂   ○ 🙂

CRAVINGS / RESPONSE

Something to make tomorrow better:

DAY (33)

BREAKFAST

LUNCH

DINNER

SNACKS

WATER

🥛🥛🥛🥛🥛🥛🥛🥛🥛🥛🥛🥛🥛🥛🥛🥛

SLEEP TIME

EXERCISE / ACTIVITY

How I feel today about my
food & exercise

○ ☹   ○ ☹

○ 😐   ○ 😐

○ 🙂   ○ 🙂

CRAVINGS / RESPONSE

Something to make tomorrow better:

DAY  34

BREAKFAST

LUNCH

DINNER

SNACKS

WATER

SLEEP TIME

EXERCISE / ACTIVITY

How I feel today about my
food & exercise

CRAVINGS / RESPONSE

Something to make tomorrow better:

DAY (35)

BREAKFAST

_____
_____
_____
_____

SNACKS

_____
_____
_____

LUNCH

_____
_____
_____
_____
_____
_____
_____
_____

DINNER

_____
_____
_____
_____

WATER

🥛🥛🥛🥛🥛🥛🥛🥛🥛🥛🥛🥛🥛🥛🥛🥛🥛

SLEEP TIME

_____

EXERCISE / ACTIVITY

_____
_____
_____
_____

How I feel today about my
food & exercise

○ 🙁   ○ 🙁
○ 😐   ○ 😐
○ 🙂   ○ 🙂

CRAVINGS / RESPONSE

_____
_____

Something to make tomorrow better:

_____
_____

DAY  36

BREAKFAST

LUNCH

DINNER

SNACKS

WATER

𐃗𐃗𐃗𐃗𐃗𐃗𐃗𐃗𐃗𐃗𐃗𐃗𐃗𐃗𐃗𐃗

SLEEP TIME

EXERCISE / ACTIVITY

How I feel today about my
food & exercise

○ ☹   ○ ☹

○ 😐   ○ 😐

○ ☺   ○ ☺

CRAVINGS / RESPONSE

Something to make tomorrow better:

DAY

BREAKFAST   LUNCH   DINNER

SNACKS

WATER   SLEEP TIME

EXERCISE / ACTIVITY

How I feel today about my
food   &   exercise

o 🙁   o 🙁

o 😐   o 😐

o 🙂   o 🙂

CRAVINGS / RESPONSE

Something to make tomorrow better:

DAY  38

BREAKFAST   LUNCH   DINNER

....
....
....
....

SNACKS
                          ....
....
....
....
....

WATER   SLEEP TIME

⊔ ⊔ ⊔ ⊔ ⊔ ⊔ ⊔ ⊔ ⊔ ⊔ ⊔ ⊔ ⊔ ⊔ ⊔ ⊔   ....

EXERCISE / ACTIVITY

....   How I feel today about my
....   food   &   exercise
....
....   ○ ☹   ○ ☹
....
                                                    ○ 😐   ○ 😐

                                                    ○ ☺   ○ ☺

CRAVINGS / RESPONSE

....
....

Something to make tomorrow better:

....
....

DAY (39)

BREAKFAST   LUNCH   DINNER

_____   _____   _____

_____   _____   _____

_____   _____   _____

_____   _____   _____

SNACKS

_____   _____   _____

_____   _____   _____

_____   _____   _____

_____   _____   _____

WATER   SLEEP TIME

[glasses icons]   _____

EXERCISE / ACTIVITY

_____   How I feel today about my
                                                 food   &   exercise
_____
                                             ○ 🙁   ○ 🙁
_____
                                             ○ 😐   ○ 😐
_____
                                             ○ 🙂   ○ 🙂

CRAVINGS / RESPONSE

_____

_____

Something to make tomorrow better:

_____

_____

DAY  40

BREAKFAST   LUNCH   DINNER

SNACKS

WATER

〇〇〇〇〇〇〇〇〇〇〇〇〇〇〇〇〇〇

SLEEP TIME

EXERCISE / ACTIVITY

How I feel today about my
food & exercise

o ☹   o ☹
o 😐   o 😐
o 🙂   o 🙂

CRAVINGS / RESPONSE

Something to make tomorrow better:

DAY (41)

BREAKFAST

LUNCH

DINNER

SNACKS

WATER

♡♡♡♡♡♡♡♡♡♡♡♡♡♡♡♡

SLEEP TIME

EXERCISE / ACTIVITY

How I feel today about my
food & exercise

○ (︶︶)   ○ (︶︶)

○ (⊙⊙)   ○ (⊙⊙)

○ (◡◡)   ○ (◡◡)

CRAVINGS / RESPONSE

Something to make tomorrow better:

DAY  42

BREAKFAST   LUNCH   DINNER

_____   _____ _____

_____   _____ _____

_____   _____ _____

_____   _____ _____

SNACKS   _____

_____   _____

_____   _____

_____   _____

WATER   SLEEP TIME

🥛🥛🥛🥛🥛🥛🥛🥛🥛🥛🥛🥛🥛🥛🥛🥛🥛🥛   _____

EXERCISE / ACTIVITY

_____   How I feel today about my
_____   food   &   exercise
_____
_____   ○ ☹   ○ ☹

_____   ○ 😐   ○ 😐

CRAVINGS / RESPONSE   ○ ☺   ○ ☺

_____

_____

Something to make tomorrow better:

_____

_____

DAY (43)

BREAKFAST

LUNCH

DINNER

SNACKS

WATER

🥛🥛🥛🥛🥛🥛🥛🥛🥛🥛🥛🥛🥛🥛🥛🥛🥛

SLEEP TIME

EXERCISE / ACTIVITY

How I feel today about my
food & exercise

○ ☹   ○ ☹

○ 😐   ○ 😐

○ 🙂   ○ 🙂

CRAVINGS / RESPONSE

Something to make tomorrow better:

DAY

BREAKFAST
LUNCH
DINNER

SNACKS

WATER
SLEEP TIME

EXERCISE / ACTIVITY

How I feel today about my
food & exercise

○ ☹   ○ ☹

○ 😐   ○ 😐

○ ☺   ○ ☺

CRAVINGS / RESPONSE

Something to make tomorrow better:

DAY (45)

BREAKFAST

....
....
....
....

SNACKS

....
....
....

LUNCH

....
....
....
....
....
....
....
....

DINNER

....
....
....
....

WATER

⊔⊔⊔⊔⊔⊔⊔⊔⊔⊔⊔⊔⊔⊔⊔⊔⊔⊔

EXERCISE / ACTIVITY

....
....
....
....

SLEEP TIME

....

How I feel today about my
food & exercise

○ ☹   ○ ☹
○ 😐   ○ 😐
○ ☺   ○ ☺

CRAVINGS / RESPONSE

....
....

Something to make tomorrow better:

....
....

DAY (46)

BREAKFAST

LUNCH

DINNER

SNACKS

WATER

🥛🥛🥛🥛🥛🥛🥛🥛🥛🥛🥛🥛🥛🥛🥛🥛

EXERCISE / ACTIVITY

SLEEP TIME

How I feel today about my
food & exercise

○ ☹   ○ ☹

○ 😐   ○ 😐

○ ☺   ○ ☺

CRAVINGS / RESPONSE

Something to make tomorrow better:

DAY (47)

BREAKFAST

LUNCH

DINNER

SNACKS

WATER

SLEEP TIME

EXERCISE / ACTIVITY

How I feel today about my
food & exercise

○ ☹ ○ ☹
○ 😐 ○ 😐
○ ☺ ○ ☺

CRAVINGS / RESPONSE

Something to make tomorrow better:

DAY (48)

BREAKFAST

_____
_____
_____
_____

SNACKS

_____
_____
_____
_____

LUNCH

_____
_____
_____
_____
_____
_____
_____
_____

DINNER

_____
_____
_____
_____
_____
_____
_____

WATER

SLEEP TIME

_____

EXERCISE / ACTIVITY

_____
_____
_____
_____
_____

How I feel today about my food & exercise

food:
○ ☹
○ 😐
○ ☺

exercise:
○ ☹
○ 😐
○ ☺

CRAVINGS / RESPONSE

_____
_____

Something to make tomorrow better:

_____
_____

DAY (49)

BREAKFAST

_____
_____
_____
_____

LUNCH

_____
_____
_____
_____

DINNER

_____
_____
_____
_____

SNACKS

_____
_____
_____
_____

WATER

🥛🥛🥛🥛🥛🥛🥛🥛🥛🥛🥛🥛🥛🥛🥛🥛

EXERCISE / ACTIVITY

_____
_____
_____
_____

SLEEP TIME

_____

How I feel today about my
food   &   exercise

○ ☹   ○ ☹
○ 😐   ○ 😐
○ ☺   ○ ☺

CRAVINGS / RESPONSE

_____

Something to make tomorrow better:

_____
_____

DAY  50

BREAKFAST

....
....
....

SNACKS

....
....
....

LUNCH

....
....
....
....
....
....
....

DINNER

....
....
....
....
....
....
....

WATER

SLEEP TIME

....

EXERCISE / ACTIVITY

....
....
....
....

How I feel today about my food & exercise

food
○ ☹
○ 😐
○ ☺

exercise
○ ☹
○ 😐
○ ☺

CRAVINGS / RESPONSE

....
....

Something to make tomorrow better:

....
....

DAY (51)

BREAKFAST

LUNCH

DINNER

SNACKS

WATER

SLEEP TIME

EXERCISE / ACTIVITY

How I feel today about my
food & exercise

○ ☹   ○ ☹

○ 😐   ○ 😐

○ ☺   ○ ☺

CRAVINGS / RESPONSE

Something to make tomorrow better:

DAY

BREAKFAST

LUNCH

DINNER

SNACKS

WATER

SLEEP TIME

EXERCISE / ACTIVITY

How I feel today about my
food & exercise

CRAVINGS / RESPONSE

Something to make tomorrow better:

DAY (53)

BREAKFAST

_____
_____
_____
_____

LUNCH

_____
_____
_____
_____

DINNER

_____
_____
_____
_____

SNACKS

_____
_____
_____
_____

WATER

☐☐☐☐☐☐☐☐☐☐☐☐☐☐☐☐

SLEEP TIME

_____

EXERCISE / ACTIVITY

_____
_____
_____
_____

How I feel today about my food & exercise

○ ☹   ○ ☹
○ 😐   ○ 😐
○ ☺   ○ ☺

CRAVINGS / RESPONSE

_____

Something to make tomorrow better:

_____
_____

DAY

BREAKFAST

LUNCH

DINNER

SNACKS

WATER

SLEEP TIME

EXERCISE / ACTIVITY

How I feel today about my
food & exercise

CRAVINGS / RESPONSE

Something to make tomorrow better:

DAY (55)

BREAKFAST

....
....
....
....

LUNCH

....
....
....
....

DINNER

....
....
....
....

SNACKS

....
....
....
....

WATER

🥛🥛🥛🥛🥛🥛🥛🥛🥛🥛🥛🥛🥛🥛🥛🥛

EXERCISE / ACTIVITY

....
....
....

SLEEP TIME

....

How I feel today about my food & exercise

○ ☹   ○ ☹
○ 😐   ○ 😐
○ ☺   ○ ☺

CRAVINGS / RESPONSE

....
....

Something to make tomorrow better:

....
....

DAY  56

BREAKFAST　　　　LUNCH　　　　　DINNER

SNACKS

WATER

SLEEP TIME

EXERCISE / ACTIVITY

How I feel today about my
food　&　exercise

○ ☹　　　○ ☹

○ 😐　　　○ 😐

○ ☺　　　○ ☺

CRAVINGS / RESPONSE

Something to make tomorrow better:

DAY

BREAKFAST

LUNCH

DINNER

SNACKS

WATER

SLEEP TIME

EXERCISE / ACTIVITY

How I feel today about my
food   &   exercise

○ ☹   ○ ☹

○ 😐   ○ 😐

○ ☺   ○ ☺

CRAVINGS / RESPONSE

Something to make tomorrow better:

DAY

BREAKFAST   LUNCH   DINNER

_____   _____   _____
_____   _____   _____
_____   _____   _____

SNACKS   _____   _____

_____   _____   _____
_____   _____   _____
_____   _____   _____

WATER   SLEEP TIME

(water glasses)   _____

EXERCISE / ACTIVITY

_____   How I feel today about my
_____   food & exercise
_____   ○ :(○ :(
_____   ○ :| ○ :|
_____   ○ :)   ○ :)

CRAVINGS / RESPONSE

_____
_____

Something to make tomorrow better:

_____
_____

DAY (59)

BREAKFAST   LUNCH   DINNER

SNACKS

WATER
□□□□□□□□□□□□□□□□□□

SLEEP TIME

EXERCISE / ACTIVITY

How I feel today about my
food   &   exercise

○ ☹   ○ ☹

○ 😐   ○ 😐

○ ☺   ○ ☺

CRAVINGS / RESPONSE

Something to make tomorrow better:

DAY  60

BREAKFAST	LUNCH	DINNER

SNACKS

WATER

🥤🥤🥤🥤🥤🥤🥤🥤🥤🥤🥤🥤🥤🥤🥤🥤

SLEEP TIME

EXERCISE / ACTIVITY

How I feel today about my
food & exercise

○ 🙁   ○ 🙁

○ 😐   ○ 😐

○ 🙂   ○ 🙂

CRAVINGS / RESPONSE

Something to make tomorrow better:

DAY 61

BREAKFAST

LUNCH

DINNER

SNACKS

WATER

🥤🥤🥤🥤🥤🥤🥤🥤🥤🥤🥤🥤🥤🥤🥤🥤

EXERCISE / ACTIVITY

SLEEP TIME

How I feel today about my
food & exercise

○ ☹   ○ ☹

○ 😐   ○ 😐

○ 🙂   ○ 🙂

CRAVINGS / RESPONSE

Something to make tomorrow better:

DAY  62

BREAKFAST   LUNCH   DINNER

_____   _____   _____

_____   _____   _____

_____   _____   _____

_____   _____   _____

SNACKS   _____   _____

_____   _____   _____

_____   _____   _____

_____   _____   _____

WATER   SLEEP TIME

🥛🥛🥛🥛🥛🥛🥛🥛🥛🥛🥛🥛🥛🥛🥛🥛   _____

EXERCISE / ACTIVITY

_____   How I feel today about my
                                                      food & exercise
_____

_____   ○ ☹   ○ ☹

_____   ○ 😐   ○ 😐

_____   ○ ☺   ○ ☺

CRAVINGS / RESPONSE

_____

_____

Something to make tomorrow better:

_____

_____

DAY (63)

BREAKFAST
....
....
....
....

LUNCH
....
....
....
....

DINNER
....
....
....
....

SNACKS
....
....
....
....

WATER

⊔⊔⊔⊔⊔⊔⊔⊔⊔⊔⊔⊔⊔⊔⊔⊔⊔⊔⊔⊔

SLEEP TIME
....

EXERCISE / ACTIVITY
....
....
....
....

How I feel today about my
food & exercise

○ :(○ :(

○ :| ○ :|

○ :)   ○ :)

CRAVINGS / RESPONSE
....

Something to make tomorrow better:
....
....

DAY (64)

BREAKFAST

_____
_____
_____
_____

SNACKS

_____
_____
_____

LUNCH

_____
_____
_____
_____
_____
_____
_____

DINNER

_____
_____
_____
_____
_____
_____
_____

WATER

🥛🥛🥛🥛🥛🥛🥛🥛🥛🥛🥛🥛🥛🥛🥛🥛

EXERCISE / ACTIVITY

_____
_____
_____
_____

SLEEP TIME

_____

How I feel today about my
food   &   exercise

○ ☹   ○ ☹
○ 😐   ○ 😐
○ ☺   ○ ☺

CRAVINGS / RESPONSE

_____

Something to make tomorrow better:

_____
_____

DAY (65)

BREAKFAST

....
....
....
....

LUNCH

....
....
....
....

DINNER

....
....
....
....

SNACKS

....
....
....
....

WATER

🥛🥛🥛🥛🥛🥛🥛🥛🥛🥛🥛🥛🥛🥛🥛🥛

EXERCISE / ACTIVITY

....
....
....
....

SLEEP TIME

....

How I feel today about my
food   &   exercise

o ☹   o ☹
o 😐   o 😐
o ☺   o ☺

CRAVINGS / RESPONSE

....
....

Something to make tomorrow better:

....
....

DAY  66

BREAKFAST	LUNCH	DINNER
....	....	....
....	....	....
....	....	....
....	....	....

SNACKS

....

....

....

....

WATER

🥛🥛🥛🥛🥛🥛🥛🥛🥛🥛🥛🥛🥛🥛🥛🥛🥛🥛

SLEEP TIME

....

EXERCISE / ACTIVITY

....

....

....

....

How I feel today about my food & exercise

○ 🙁   ○ 🙁

○ 😐   ○ 😐

○ 🙂   ○ 🙂

CRAVINGS / RESPONSE

....

....

Something to make tomorrow better:

....

....

DAY (67)

BREAKFAST

LUNCH

DINNER

SNACKS

WATER

SLEEP TIME

EXERCISE / ACTIVITY

How I feel today about my
food & exercise

o (☹)   o (☹)

o (😐)   o (😐)

o (☺)   o (☺)

CRAVINGS / RESPONSE

Something to make tomorrow better:

DAY

BREAKFAST   LUNCH   DINNER

SNACKS

WATER   SLEEP TIME

🥛🥛🥛🥛🥛🥛🥛🥛🥛🥛🥛🥛🥛🥛🥛🥛

EXERCISE / ACTIVITY

How I feel today about my
food & exercise

○ ☹   ○ ☹

○ 😐   ○ 😐

○ 🙂   ○ 🙂

CRAVINGS / RESPONSE

Something to make tomorrow better:

DAY (69)

BREAKFAST

....
....
....
....

LUNCH

....
....
....
....

DINNER

....
....
....
....

SNACKS

....
....
....

WATER

⊔⊔⊔⊔⊔⊔⊔⊔⊔⊔⊔⊔⊔⊔⊔⊔

EXERCISE / ACTIVITY

....
....
....

SLEEP TIME

....

How I feel today about my food & exercise

○ ☹   ○ ☹
○ 😐   ○ 😐
○ ☺   ○ ☺

CRAVINGS / RESPONSE

....

Something to make tomorrow better:

....
....

DAY

BREAKFAST   LUNCH   DINNER

....

....

....

....

SNACKS

....

....

....

WATER

SLEEP TIME

EXERCISE / ACTIVITY

How I feel today about my
food   &   exercise

○ 😟   ○ 😟

○ 😐   ○ 😐

○ 🙂   ○ 🙂

CRAVINGS / RESPONSE

Something to make tomorrow better:

DAY

BREAKFAST   LUNCH   DINNER

....

....

....

SNACKS   ....

....

....

....

WATER   SLEEP TIME

🥛🥛🥛🥛🥛🥛🥛🥛🥛🥛🥛🥛🥛🥛🥛🥛   ....

EXERCISE / ACTIVITY

....   How I feel today about my
                                           food   &   exercise
....
                                      ○ 🙁   ○ 🙁
....
                                      ○ 😐   ○ 😐
....
                                      ○ 🙂   ○ 🙂

CRAVINGS / RESPONSE

....

....

Something to make tomorrow better:

....

....

DAY

BREAKFAST   LUNCH   DINNER

SNACKS

WATER   SLEEP TIME

EXERCISE / ACTIVITY

How I feel today about my
food & exercise

○ ☹   ○ ☹

○ 😐   ○ 😐

○ 🙂   ○ 🙂

CRAVINGS / RESPONSE

Something to make tomorrow better:

DAY (73)

BREAKFAST   LUNCH   DINNER

....

....

....

SNACKS   ....

....

....

....

....

WATER   SLEEP TIME

🥛🥛🥛🥛🥛🥛🥛🥛🥛🥛🥛🥛🥛🥛🥛🥛🥛🥛 ....

EXERCISE / ACTIVITY

.... How I feel today about my
                                                        food & exercise
....

....   ○ ☹   ○ ☹

....   ○ 😐   ○ 😐

....   ○ ☺   ○ ☺

CRAVINGS / RESPONSE

....

....

Something to make tomorrow better:

....

....

DAY  74

BREAKFAST   LUNCH   DINNER

....

....

....

....

SNACKS   ....

....

....

....

WATER   SLEEP TIME

EXERCISE / ACTIVITY

....

....   How I feel today about my
                                                                                food & exercise
....

....   ○ ☹   ○ ☹

....   ○ 😐   ○ 😐

CRAVINGS / RESPONSE   ○ 🙂   ○ 🙂

....

....

Something to make tomorrow better:

....

....

DAY  75

BREAKFAST   LUNCH   DINNER

_____ _____ _____
_____ _____ _____
_____ _____ _____
_____ _____ _____

SNACKS   _____ _____
_____ _____ _____
_____ _____ _____
_____ _____ _____

WATER   SLEEP TIME

(water glasses)   _____

EXERCISE / ACTIVITY

_____   How I feel today about my
_____   food & exercise
_____
_____   ○ ☹   ○ ☹
_____
                                                  ○ 😐   ○ 😐

                                                  ○ ☺   ○ ☺

CRAVINGS / RESPONSE

_____
_____

Something to make tomorrow better:

_____
_____

DAY

BREAKFAST   LUNCH   DINNER

....
....
....
....

SNACKS

....
....
....
....

WATER   SLEEP TIME

🥛🥛🥛🥛🥛🥛🥛🥛🥛🥛🥛🥛🥛🥛🥛🥛   ....

EXERCISE / ACTIVITY

....   How I feel today about my
....   food & exercise
....
....   ○ ☹   ○ ☹
....   ○ 😐   ○ 😐
                                                  ○ ☺   ○ ☺

CRAVINGS / RESPONSE

....
....

Something to make tomorrow better:

....
....

DAY

BREAKFAST

LUNCH

DINNER

SNACKS

WATER

SLEEP TIME

EXERCISE / ACTIVITY

How I feel today about my
food & exercise

○ 🙁   ○ 🙁

○ 😐   ○ 😐

○ 🙂   ○ 🙂

CRAVINGS / RESPONSE

Something to make tomorrow better:

DAY

BREAKFAST   LUNCH   DINNER

....

....

....

SNACKS
....

....

....

....

WATER   SLEEP TIME
                                                     ....

EXERCISE / ACTIVITY

....   How I feel today about my
....   food   &   exercise
....
....   ○ ☹   ○ ☹
....
....   ○ 😐   ○ 😐

CRAVINGS / RESPONSE   ○ ☺   ○ ☺

....

....

Something to make tomorrow better:

....

....

DAY

BREAKFAST   LUNCH   DINNER

SNACKS

WATER

SLEEP TIME

EXERCISE / ACTIVITY

How I feel today about my
food & exercise

○ ☹   ○ ☹

○ 😐   ○ 😐

○ ☺   ○ ☺

CRAVINGS / RESPONSE

Something to make tomorrow better:

DAY  80

BREAKFAST   LUNCH   DINNER

_____   _____   _____

_____   _____   _____

_____   _____   _____

_____   _____   _____

SNACKS   _____   _____

_____   _____   _____

_____   _____   _____

_____   _____   _____

WATER   SLEEP TIME

🥛🥛🥛🥛🥛🥛🥛🥛🥛🥛🥛🥛🥛🥛🥛🥛   _____

EXERCISE / ACTIVITY

_____   How I feel today about my
                                food & exercise
_____

_____   ○ ☹   ○ ☹

_____   ○ 😐   ○ 😐

_____   ○ ☺   ○ ☺

CRAVINGS / RESPONSE

_____

_____

Something to make tomorrow better:

_____

_____

DAY (81)

BREAKFAST

_____
_____
_____
_____

LUNCH

_____
_____
_____
_____

DINNER

_____
_____
_____
_____

SNACKS

_____
_____
_____
_____

WATER

🥛🥛🥛🥛🥛🥛🥛🥛🥛🥛🥛🥛🥛🥛🥛🥛

EXERCISE / ACTIVITY

_____
_____
_____
_____

SLEEP TIME

_____

How I feel today about my
food & exercise

food:
○ ☹
○ 😐
○ ☺

exercise:
○ ☹
○ 😐
○ ☺

CRAVINGS / RESPONSE

_____
_____

Something to make tomorrow better:

_____
_____

DAY  82

BREAKFAST	LUNCH	DINNER
....	....	....
....	....	....
....	....	....
....	....	....

SNACKS

WATER

🥛🥛🥛🥛🥛🥛🥛🥛🥛🥛🥛🥛🥛🥛🥛🥛

SLEEP TIME

EXERCISE / ACTIVITY

How I feel today about my food & exercise

○ ☹   ○ ☹
○ 😐   ○ 😐
○ 🙂   ○ 🙂

CRAVINGS / RESPONSE

Something to make tomorrow better:

DAY (83)

BREAKFAST

_____
_____
_____
_____

SNACKS

_____
_____
_____

LUNCH

_____
_____
_____
_____
_____
_____
_____

DINNER

_____
_____
_____
_____

WATER

🥛🥛🥛🥛🥛🥛🥛🥛🥛🥛🥛🥛🥛🥛🥛🥛

EXERCISE / ACTIVITY

_____
_____
_____

SLEEP TIME

_____

How I feel today about my
food & exercise

o ☹   o ☹
o 😐   o 😐
o ☺   o ☺

CRAVINGS / RESPONSE

_____

Something to make tomorrow better:

_____
_____

DAY  84

BREAKFAST   LUNCH   DINNER

_____   _____   _____
_____   _____   _____
_____   _____   _____

SNACKS

_____   _____   _____
_____   _____   _____
_____   _____   _____

WATER   SLEEP TIME

🥛🥛🥛🥛🥛🥛🥛🥛🥛🥛🥛🥛🥛🥛🥛🥛   _____

EXERCISE / ACTIVITY

                                       How I feel today about my
_____   food & exercise
_____   ○ ☹   ○ ☹
_____   ○ 😐   ○ 😐
_____   ○ 🙂   ○ 🙂

CRAVINGS / RESPONSE

_____
_____

Something to make tomorrow better:

_____
_____

DAY (85)

BREAKFAST

_____
_____
_____
_____

LUNCH

_____
_____
_____
_____

DINNER

_____
_____
_____
_____

SNACKS

_____
_____
_____
_____

WATER

SLEEP TIME

_____

EXERCISE / ACTIVITY

_____
_____
_____

How I feel today about my
food & exercise

o 😟   o 😟
o 😐   o 😐
o 🙂   o 🙂

CRAVINGS / RESPONSE

_____

Something to make tomorrow better:

_____
_____

DAY  86

BREAKFAST   LUNCH   DINNER

_____   _____   _____
_____   _____   _____
_____   _____   _____
_____   _____   _____

SNACKS   _____   _____

_____   _____   _____
_____   _____   _____
_____   _____   _____

WATER   SLEEP TIME

EXERCISE / ACTIVITY

_____

_____

_____   How I feel today about my
                                                food & exercise

_____   ○ ☹   ○ ☹

_____   ○ 😐   ○ 😐

                                            ○ ☺   ○ ☺

CRAVINGS / RESPONSE

_____

_____

Something to make tomorrow better:

_____

_____

DAY (87)

BREAKFAST

_____
_____
_____
_____

LUNCH

_____
_____
_____
_____

DINNER

_____
_____
_____
_____

SNACKS

_____
_____
_____
_____

WATER

▢▢▢▢▢▢▢▢▢▢▢▢▢▢▢▢▢▢

EXERCISE / ACTIVITY

_____
_____
_____
_____

SLEEP TIME

_____

How I feel today about my
food & exercise

o 😟   o 😟
o 😐   o 😐
o 🙂   o 🙂

CRAVINGS / RESPONSE

_____

Something to make tomorrow better:

_____
_____

DAY  88

BREAKFAST

LUNCH

DINNER

SNACKS

WATER

SLEEP TIME

EXERCISE / ACTIVITY

How I feel today about my
food & exercise

CRAVINGS / RESPONSE

Something to make tomorrow better:

DAY (89)

BREAKFAST

....
....
....
....

LUNCH

....
....
....
....

DINNER

....
....
....
....

SNACKS

....
....
....
....

WATER

⬜⬜⬜⬜⬜⬜⬜⬜⬜⬜⬜⬜⬜⬜⬜⬜

SLEEP TIME

....

EXERCISE / ACTIVITY

....
....
....

How I feel today about my
food & exercise

○ 🙁   ○ 🙁
○ 😐   ○ 😐
○ 🙂   ○ 🙂

CRAVINGS / RESPONSE

....

Something to make tomorrow better:

....
....

DAY 90

BREAKFAST

LUNCH

DINNER

SNACKS

WATER

🥛🥛🥛🥛🥛🥛🥛🥛🥛🥛🥛🥛🥛🥛🥛🥛

SLEEP TIME

EXERCISE / ACTIVITY

How I feel today about my
food   &   exercise

o 😞   o 😞

o 😐   o 😐

o 🙂   o 🙂

CRAVINGS / RESPONSE

Something to make tomorrow better:

DAY 90 : Hello New Me!

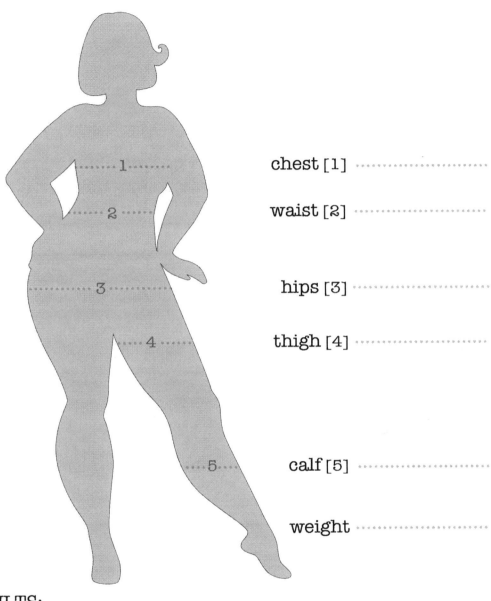

chest [1] ·······························

waist [2] ·······························

hips [3] ·······························

thigh [4] ·······························

calf [5] ·······························

weight ·······························

RESULTS:

I am still gorgeous! Habits to keep, things to improve: ·······················

···

···

···

Hey, Gorgeous!

The book you have in your hands is brought to you by Happy Books Hub. We have a passion for creating books that can improve and add joy to people's lives. Hopefully this journal will accomplish just that for you!

If you have any suggestions on how to improve it, or what we can change or add to make it more useful particularly to you, please don't hesitate to contact us at **happybookshub@gmail.com**
We would be more than happy to consider how to apply your suggestion to this journal's next edition.

Thank you for buying Hello New Me journal!

Please, support us and leave a review!

Love,
Happy Books Hub

Made in the USA
Middletown, DE
16 October 2018